Making Costumes for Plays

JOAN PETERS AND ANNA SUTCLIFFE

BT Batsford Ltd   *London*

Acknowledgment

The authors would like to thank the following for their help and encouragement: The Chief Education Officer of Leeds; Miss J. Harland, Principal of the James Graham College, Leeds; Mrs A. Sugden, Headmistress of West Park County Secondary School for Girls, Leeds; the staff and students of the James Graham College, especially the students in the Main and Subsidiary Art and Main English Courses, and the pupils of West Park School. Also Malcolm Sunderland, Terence Shannon and Anne Mosedale for their great practical help during the preparation of the book.

Acknowledgment and thanks are also due to Edward Grinham and his students for taking the majority of the photographs, and to Jerry Bird for photograph on page 76 right; Philip Clemishaw for photographs page 21 right, page 79, and page 84 left; Howard Fountain for photograph page 32 left; Ted Grinham for photographs on pages 19, 20 right, 23, 26 left, 29, 31, 44 right, 45, 50, 51, 52, 53, 59 right, 60 right and top left, 61 bottom, 62, 63, 68, 70 right, 76 left, and 90; Alan Gummerson for photographs page 9 left, and page 34 bottom right; John Henstock for photographs on pages 7, 11, and 88 bottom; Keith Tones for photograph on page 77; and the Yorkshire Evening Post for photographs on pages 21 bottom right, 80 top, and 86 bottom left.

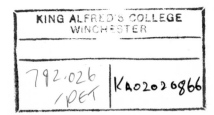
© *Joan Peters and Anna Sutcliffe 1970 and 1977*
First published 1970
New edition 1977

ISBN 0 7134 0029 3

Filmset in 11 on 12 point Monophoto Apollo
by Servis Filmsetting Ltd, Manchester
Printed and bound by
The Anchor Press Ltd, Tiptree, Essex
for the Publishers
B T Batsford Limited
4 Fitzhardinge Street, London W1H 0AH

Contents

Introduction

To those who are committed to the serious production of plays and related activities, whether in education or for personal fulfilment, maybe it comes as a surprise that the excitement of creating in form and colour in costume, as well as through words, movement lighting and sets, should so often be ignored.

Costumes are sometimes regarded simply as a chore, to be given to an overburdened needlecraft department, or they are hired; the players being at the mercy of the costume hirers and subject to the availability of certain garments. In such cases, costumes can often be splendid but inconsistent, particularly if they are left over from professional productions in large theatres, as they usually go ill with the modest resources of school or amateur companies.

There is no reason why costumes made for amateur or school productions should be less stylish than those produced with all the resources of money and skill that the professional stage affords, they may even be more so. One often has the feeling that the availability of synthetic metallic fabrics sometimes goes to the head of many professional designers, often resulting in something unsuitable and meretricious.

The important thing is to be rational and imaginative in the management of resources and it helps if even the simplest visual effects are achieved in a really serious spirit.

We do not underestimate the value of expert cutting and craftsmanship in the making of costumes. Many books exist on the history of costume and on cutting and sewing, including the correct patterns of period costume. But we are concerned here rather to extend the scope of the work and to show how a very wide range of creative activity and improvisation can contribute in a school or other learning situation, as our methods can give opportunity for imaginative work to more participants. For those daunted by lack of expertise in cutting and sewing, we offer various suggestions for simple methods of construction. We are not at all in favour of fashionable gimmicks, as distinct from really creative re-thinking, we believe strongly in the need to evoke for instance the characteristic style of a period, but we believe that the stage performance is an illusion, and that the mere slavish copying of the details of a period is not the most important thing.

Costume design in schools is not necessarily comparable to that in either the professional or amateur theatre where the work of a creative designer will usually in the former and hopefully in the latter, be faithfully interpreted, and the actual task of making will afford little or no individual opportunity for the maker. In an educational situation there must be scope for the individual to contribute, and this is one of the reasons why we suggest that costume plays (all things being equal), sometimes have the greatest educational value.

We are aware that much thinking is going on about the place of drama and threatre in the curriculum, and their relationships to other areas of study. We have every sympathy with the efforts being made to develop the awareness of children through improvisation, mime, role-play and regular work in the classroom, but we are convinced that the production of plays, and/or works involving music and dance, as complete works of art involving many creative contributions, should not be abandoned. There is no reason why that texts used should not themselves be the result of earlier creative thinking, and group composition techniques.

School productions must surely be regarded as serious occasions for learning, not least about the discipline and dedication necessary for the creation of art.

There are several philosophies of amateur stage production. Some groups regard their task as being to produce a finished and polished artefact with great devotion to the text or score, others believe their dramatic activities to be occasions for 'group dynamics', for finding out about people. Yet others are concerned to help to increase participation. We sympathise with these activities and are interested in them all, though perhaps we are here most concerned with 'amateur' theatre and theatre in education as an attempt to understand a text through the production of it as a work of art.

Tabard in dyed hessian and gold painted fabric scraps, with free appliqué and metallic items, worn over jumpers and tights

7

Materials

REMEMBER, NEVER THROW ANYTHING AWAY!
Some useful items for collection
Old sheets, blankets, curtains, bedspreads
Old evening and cocktail dresses (often found at jumble sales)
Tray cloths, lace table cloths, all kinds of braid, and crochet edging
Lace, ribbon, fringing, frills, seams and edging
Old and broken costume jewelry, beads, feathers, broken mirror, coloured glass
Lead foil from wine bottle tops, any small metal articles (screws, nuts, paper clips) tin lids, beer bottle tops
Plastic articles, particularly polythene lids, various cartons, bottle stoppers
Scraps of fur and leather
Shoes and high boots
Felt and straw hats
Sacks and sacking
Shirts, especially white or plain colours
Jumpers and cardigans, socks (three quarter white ones are especially useful for eighteenth century plays), heavy tights, thick coloured stockings, old trousers of all kinds

Suggested new materials
In addition to cheap, unbleached calico, or other cheap fabric, you may need new material. If so, furnishing remnants, often half price, are much the best buy, being usually wider and heavier than dress fabric at the same price. Take care however, because some of the thinner modern rayons hang and light badly, and are difficult to use for period costumes. When buying wool, sale bargains in dress and coat fabrics are sometimes available, and tubular jersey wool is a good investment. Nothing surpasses wool.

Suppliers

Helizarin dye and Binder D
55–7 Glengall Road,
London SE15 6NQ

Printex (Tinolite) and Binder CM
Brico Commercial Chemical Co. Ltd
Winsor and Newton
Education Division, Wealdstone, Harrow
Middlesex
Geigy (UK) Limited, 42 Berkeley Square
London W1 *and*
Simonsway, Manchester 22

Dylon and Procion dyes
Mayborne Products Limited
139–47 Sydenham Road, London SE26

Metallic powder and aniline dyes
Brodie and Middleton
74 Long Acre, London WC2

Marvin Medium and school art supplies
Margros Limited
Monument House Monument Way West
Woking, Surrey

Paraffin wax
The Hygenol Company Ltd
Rothwell-Haigh, Leeds, Yorks

The work illustrated in this book is printed with *Helizarin* or printer's ink but any pigment printing process such as *Tinolite/Printex, Polyprint, Bedafin,* etc. may be used. All dyeing is done with *Dylon, Procion* or cheap aniline dyes, although any other home dyes are suitable.

ABOVE *Jane and the 'bit box'*

TOP RIGHT *Feathers, metal waste, beads*

ABOVE RIGHT *Feathers, seed pods and other useful items*

Cheap fabrics and remnants
Bradley Textiles Ltd
15 Stott Street, Nelson, Lancashire

Cheap bulk fabrics and dressmakers' sundries
McCullock and Wallis
Dering Street, London W1R 0BH

Beads, stage jewels, etc
Ells and Farrier Ltd
5 Princes Street, London W1R 8PH

Sesame Ventures
Greenham Hall, Wellington, Somerset

9

Notes on style

It is important to bear in mind that all parts of a production must ideally make up a satisfying whole. A usual practice in the theatre is to have very rich costumes and properties in a very simple set. Sometimes there is no actual set at all, the backstage area being revealed, and the costumes made up during the action, from items in a hamper—a typical 'alienation effect'. Sometimes the set will be an abstract arrangement of ramps, rostra, etc with no attempt to depict an actual place. What is necessary is that the set should be constructed to help the movement and action. However, these practices should not be taken as an excuse for making set and costume that contradict one another. We once saw an exquisite set made entirely in paper sculpture, but it did not work against spun-rayon dresses. If authentic costumes are used (and quite a lot of genuine Victorian costumes may be available), remember that these were made for close scrutiny, and if all the costumes are made in the same idiom to suit them, the result may be too refined for the stage. It may be better to make everything, however desirable great-granny's cape may be. These things *can* be used and often are—we have used many original articles, especially feather boas, gloves, hats and parasols: but be aware of the problems. Sometimes children, dancing class pupils especially, have access to very well-made professionally cut historical costumes. It is often heartbreaking not to use such articles, but they should be used only if the work in school can be done in the same idiom, and with the same kind of expertise. This may well be easy for the needlecraft department, but it may inhibit other kinds of creative work.

Some parents are often most anxious to help the school, and may be prepared to rig out their children at considerable expense, but this help must be declined if the rest of the production is likely to fail to reach this standard of cut and fabric. It may be frustrating for Titania if she is firmly told that she cannot wear her tutu (the most expensive one in the ballet group at that), but it is going to be necessary if the rest of the play is in Greek costume!

Some schools, we gather, convinced that they cannot organise the work themselves, and without the money to hire costumes, simply leave each cast member to contrive a costume with the help of parents. Much fun may result, but getting any unity is difficult. In our experience, the golden rules are: start early, plan ahead, work steadily towards the goal; or improvise at the last moment with dash and simplicity. Do not rely on the school down the road; and always have a great deal of raw material about. In most cases the 'rawer' the better.

Things we would deprecate: fruit-gum jewels, baking foil, cotton wool, milk bottle tops, crêpe paper and sometimes butter-muslin.

Many schools we know do devoted work and achieve miracles. It is not always the most polished results that indicate creative thinking, but those where an inspired translation of the available material is made.

It may be thought that many of our suggestions are no more than common sense, but often for one reason or another, the departments involved rarely coordinate, and it is to help make this happen that we have planned this book.

Making up in the art room, before an evening of dance/ drama in which costumes of many periods were required. Being made up is a Charleston girl, the dress is authentic. The queue includes mediaeval lords and ladies. In the foreground is a Victorian maid wearing an authentic top (showing clearly the small size of many nineteenth century dresses), and a boy's woodwork apron with frills added. The Victorian cook on the right is similarly dressed

Basic fabrics—decorated and plain

For really good heavy draped effects, there is nothing better than old blanket. This is indeed preferable to compromising with inferior, cheap new material. This blanket brilliantly dyed, often tie-dyed or simply crumpled into the dye so as to take the colour unevenly, can give a splendid effect under stage lighting.

By far the best stand-by is old sheet and it is amazing how many of these are forthcoming when the need arises. Nothing takes dye better than old twill, especially when it is tie-dyed or blot dyed with brilliant and quite cheap aniline dyes such as those stocked by theatrical suppliers. If permanence to light and washing is essential then ordinary home dyes such as *Dylon, Drummer*, etc. may be used, or *Procion* or other re-active dyes. For the most part however school plays have short runs, and aniline dyes are cheaper and easier to use.

Heavy skirts may be made most effectively from old curtains, repp, brocade, faded velvet (this sometimes produces beautiful colours that light better than new, flat effects). Many furnishing brocades already have suitable patterns for Tudor and Renaissance costumes. If these form the basis of the design, they can be made more effective by the addition of beads and gilded cord.

To obtain texture and fresh colour on old, or cheap, plain fabrics the following materials and equipment are needed:

Polyvinyl acetate *(Marvin Medium)*
White emulsion pigment printing paste *(Helizarin Binder D* (UK), *Alizarin* (USA), *Tinolite Binder CM*, sold to schools and colleges in small quantities under the name *Printex* (UK), *Versatex* (USA))
Rubber solution
Gold, bronze or nickel-silver powder
Lino or paint rollers
25 mm or 50 mm (1 in. or 2 in.) brushes
Powder paint
Printer's ink
Turpentine substitute
Pigment dyes *(Helizarin* (UK), *Alizarin* (USA), *Acco-Lite* (USA), or *Printex (Tinolite), Versatex* (USA)).

For making a collage texture on the fabric, collect flower petals, fallen leaves, wood shavings, sawdust, fine sand, ferns, grasses, fabric shapes and scraps, beads, buttons, etc. Never throw anything away, old dyed string from tie-dyed fabrics is useful.

These may be glued at random, or in pre-arranged patterns on to the basic fabric until a rich crusty texture is obtained. The work can then be rolled flat, gold or other metallic paint and powder applied, and rolled again. This results in a varied rich texture which can be further enhanced with beads and jewels (sewn or glued), simulating the texture of fabrics featured in paintings by Rembrandt or Velasquez, rather than a slavish copy of actual textiles of the period. The slightly broken surface and contrast of light, especially if both gold and silver are used, can be most effective.

Of course if metallic fabrics are not desired, the materials can be used alone, and dye painted when the glue is dry.

If a very soft draping effect is required, we suggest painting the basic fabric with a pigment binder and metallic powder, rather than using *Marvin Medium* which will stiffen the fabric, if the pieces are then sewn by hand or machine, the result will drape well. Sewing by machine through gilded fabric is difficult, so where possible leave ungilded edges. It is impossible to machine-sew through fabric treated with *Marvin Medium*.

Yet another method of decoration, is the use of wax resist (batik), either alone or on top of existing appliqué or collage, or with collage and embroidery added (for details of batik techniques, see list of suggested books).

A good way of reproducing a pattern is to stencil melted wax through a template, subsequently cold-water dyeing the fabric. Free random painting of wax with a big brush, or drawing with a wax trailer are effective too.

Dripping paint or a mixture of paint and *Marvin Medium*, and perhaps metal powder, down the surface may be striking, alone or combined with collage and appliqué.

OPPOSITE
Leotard painted with free brush strokes, splashing and spraying. Silver, copper and gold were used on black. This and similar ones, have been used many times as a basis for costumes of fairies, witches and other supernaturals. Be careful when adapting these that back zips are concealed by drapery and decoration. Sleeves are not suitable when dressing this type of character. The mottling produces a blurred effect in movement

RIGHT *Appliqué on furnishing fabric, using scraps of various fabrics, some gold and some transparent. Also sequins, beads, plastic flower petals, etc., all freely stitched down by hand*

Screen printing, as well as painting dye through a stencil template may be used as a means of reproducing a design on fabric, this being subsequently decorated in any of the ways suggested. String collage or couching, though sometimes time-consuming, can be very attractive.

The reader will be able to think of many other interesting ways of decorating fabric. We give here the ones we have tried and found successful. Besides producing effective costumes, the creative work done on these fabrics may lead to many interesting developments in the art and craft rooms.

If paintings are used as inspiration, Venetian paintings, and the work of Rembrandt, Velasquez and Goya in particular are very helpful in inspiring textured effects, this close scrutiny will make children more familiar with the pictures. For another rich source of ideas see pictures of ancient artefacts—many are available now in colour magazines and paper backs. The rich effect of gold and jewelled objects found in tombs may very successfully be realised in a costume, as well as in actual jewelry.

ABOVE LEFT *Screen print, with additional potato printing, on dyed unbleached calico, with gold paint (powder in* Marvin Medium*), string and beads added*

CENTRE LEFT *Gold powder in* Marvin Medium *thickly applied to old cotton jersey vest, pulled, stretched, sewn, flaked, with appliqué of beads and small metal objects. Intended to simulate worn, decorated gold leather*

LEFT *Old cotton net curtain painted gold, silver and bronze (powder in Helizarin Binder D), torn and cut fabric pieces (also metalised) all appliquéd on a background of black mull, daubed with gold and silver. The original mull which was left over from a previous costume, contained some machine embroidery, the whole making a rich but soft and easily draped fabric*

ABOVE *Basic fabric of girl's dress, soft unbleached calico with poured and daubed gold and silver paint (metallic powder in* Helizarin Binder D *and* Marvin Medium*). Overskirt in rayon jersey. Boy's garment of dyed, heavy unbleached calico, with collage of braid, metalised scraps of needlecord, string, beads, etc. Yoke made from furnishing brocade, and hat of velvet and satin*

RIGHT *Houpelande of blot dyed old bedspread, richly hand appliquéd with fabric scraps, beads, jewels, etc. Lining of sleeves made from faded velvet curtain. Hat from off-cuts of same bedspread. Fur collar from our collection*

Three Kings. *Wearing from left to right: old sheet
tie-dyed in three colours with gold fabric collage added.
Chain of gold painted scrap materials and beads. Hat from
dyed sheet wound round the crown of an old hat. The second
King in tie-dyed costume with added decoration. Hat made
from old curtain fabric. Heavy collar made from tufted
carpet with applied beads and other metal objects, all
painted gold. The third King's costume was cut from a
pattern in a book on historic costume, and made from dyed
curtains. Collar made from gilded fabric with appliqué of
string, beads, etc. Gold, Frankincense and Myrrh are shown
in greater detail on page 73*

16

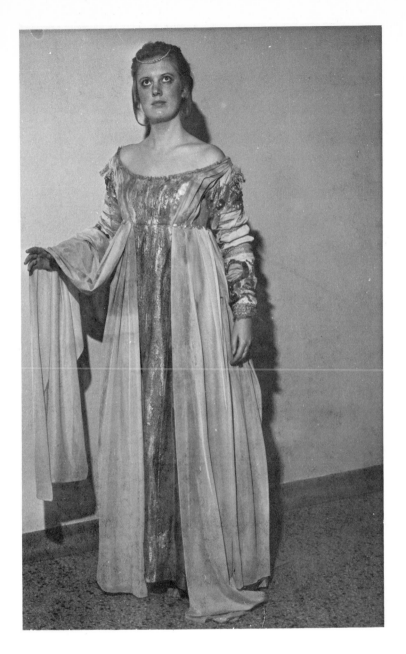

*Dress in nylon jersey, bodice made of a stretch fabric
used to facilitate rapid cast changes. The bodice is daubed
and dribbled with gold and silver paint according to our
formula, and the front in old curtain fabric similarly
treated. The skirt panels are loose, several layers deep and
of uneven length allowing graceful movement, these are
unevenly sprayed with silver, gold and bronze paint. The
sleeves contain many scraps of fabric. This dress was made
for Hermione in* A Winter's Tale, *and is basically a warm
corn colour. Yellow is referred to in the text as a symbol
of infidelity*

LEFT *Sleeveless coat over Elizabethan dress. Made from half price furnishing repp painted with gold powder in* Helizarin Binder D. *Inside faced with brocade remnants. Collage of embroidery from an old dress, hydrangea florets, fabric scraps, many old brooches and other small items of jewelry (in some cases simply pinned on), beads and sequins. This fabric is all gold, but the black of the embroidery and the various colours of some of the jewelry show through and add variety*

RIGHT *Close-up of back of coat, showing application of flower petals*

18

ABOVE TOP *Close up of front, showing embroidery taken from old evening dress*

ABOVE *Close-up of detail in the girl's skirt. This shows clearly the method of layering net, dripping gold, and collage*

RIGHT *Panel of stiff fabric made as follows: old curtain fabric thickly layered with dead leaves (not too brittle), straw, beads, etc. Glued with* Marvin Medium. *A varied metallic surface was obtained by rolling over the panel using a rubber linoleum block roller covered with gold, bronze and silver powder in* Marvin Medium. *The natural colour of the leaves occasionally shows through, and adds yet another effect. The whole simulates quite effectively, a certain kind of heavily embroidered fabric shown in Renaissance portraits. Overskirt of very cheap, blot dyed rayon taffetta*

LEFT *Early nineteenth century dress in white rayon jersey. The skirt has been added to the top of an existing dress which has been gilded and heavily worked with string, felt strips, buttons, fabric scraps, lace, beads, etc. Three shades of gold powder in Helizarin Binder D have been used, with black ink painted into some of the cracks to enhance the shadow effect. The set-in sleeves are made from tarlatan and old coat lining. The head ornament is an old metal belt sprayed bronze*

ABOVE RIGHT *The same top with sleeves removed, fitted onto a black velvet gathered skirt (substandard furnishing remnant) to make an Empire Line evening dress – a very useful basic top*

ABOVE *Doublet made from rayon furnishing fabric with heavy appliqué of fabric scraps, beads, etc., including piped velvet. Chain made from heavy cord with old buttons. Ruff made from organdie sewn with pearls. Semi-circular cloak uses scraps of velvet in panels, with satin bands freely embroidered by hand and machine. The fabric pieces are fixed down by sewing machine, ignoring raw edges which add vitality when lit. The cloak is lined with furnishing repp. This whole garment is extremely rich and heavy, illustrating the value of time and effort spent in enrichment rather than relying on the immediate effect of limp new fabric*

TOP RIGHT *Greek costume, easily made from blot dyed sheets*

RIGHT *Ragged nomad dressed in improvised costume— a piece of old blanket, showing the useful result of blot dyed fabric. The blanket was immersed in black aniline dye, which was in a small container, preventing even dyeing. We had no real control over the result, but we felt that it gave a good representation of the effect of mould on fabric*

ABOVE
Semi circular cloak in dyed blue satin cotton, with very simple raw-edge appliqué shapes fixed on by sewing machine, in dark green and scarlet. This cloak, used in a production of Tiger At The Gates *was one of several stressing bold and simple pattern in combination with highly textured dresses and dull blot dyed rags*

LEFT
Sample of heavy decoration of fabric, using tin lids, peacock feathers, large beads, charred polythene, and the whole sprayed gold. The backing is of heavy hessian, unevenly dyed. This is an example of a heavy luminous treatment which may be suitable for hangings, tabards, cloaks, armour, etc

*Cape in black coat fabric with tricel jersey bottom panel.
This combination of stiff and flexible fabric allows many
possibilities for movement. The decoration is all collage
(glued, no sewing) in red and gold fabrics and braid*

23

Panels—decorated skirts, bodices and cloaks

For people who love creative work in collage, printing, simple or complex stitchery, appliqué, hand or machine embroidery, one of the most satisfying ploys may be the making of dress panels. These, both for skirts and bodices, are particularly suitable for Renaissance plays, and especially for court characters—so Shakespeare, Beaumont and Fletcher, or Marlowe, may give many a happy hour to children who would otherwise be far from the centre of things, because of their lack of interest or ability in acting or dressmaking.

We have illustrated various ways of making these. The most appealing thing is that any and every scrap may be used—fabrics, beads, trimmings, seams, junk, string, felt scraps, etc. The effect may be carefully drawn out first and worked symmetrically, as these designs would indeed have been, or it may be a free-textured creation, aiming at an impressionistic effect. All the methods described in the chapter on the decoration of fabrics may be used, except that sometimes the panels may require the greatest detail, definition and richness because they are the focus of the costume.

If you are lucky enough to have velvet or heavy brocade for the basis of the dress, it may require no other ornament, the detail can then be supplied by sleeves, yokes and front panels, and even by cloaks and redingotes.

A dress in humbler material may need decoration all over to bring it to an equal point of glory, but the two may be combined. *The Winter's Tale* or *Love's Labour's Lost* lend themselves especially to rich decoration of this kind, and if these dresses are mixed judiciously with an occasional foil in black, or a single bright colour, the result may be very satisfying. Alternatively the richness may be the one splendid thing in a group of drab ones, and thus achieve some sort or revelatory quality.

We have made a rich ecclesiastical costume for Becket in *Murder in the Cathedral*, which stood out against priests, monks and women, thus making the character—we hoped —seem as if decked out for sacrifice.

Cloak made from old furnishing brocade, with velvet, taffetta and beads added. About six colours were used in the garment, which produces a vitality when freely organised, an effect not always achieved by slavish copying of originals

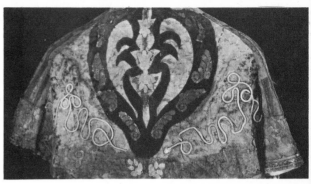

ABOVE *Back of cloak. A subtle range of black, green and bronze, with very free machine stitching with a swing needle machine. The circles at the hem of the cloak were retrieved from an old Victorian cloak which was beyond repair. The garment is finished with hanging beads*

ABOVE RIGHT *Semi-circular cloak made from blot dyed curtain, decorated with very bold collage glued onto the cloak (almost no sewing), using velvet, cotton net and soft cord, in a range of reds and oranges, all produced by dyeing. Be careful when using collage this way, not to spoil the hang of the garment by using too much glue*

Becket from Murder in the Cathedral. *Chasuble made from the skirt of an old summer dress with a convenient check pattern. This was decorated with gold brush work (powder in Helizarin Binder D) and sewn with gold painted cotton net, the garment lined with cheap red taffetta. The stole is made from felt with successive layers of felt stapled on. Many colours of felt were used, and some of these show slightly through the gold and silver paint. This item is finished with gold cord, pearl beads and theatrical jewels. The alb is cheap white cotton, trimmed with white cotton net curtain and old braid. The mitre by the same method as the stole*

ABOVE
Costume made from a velvet furnishing remnant. The panel and undersleeves are old satin, and the design entirely collage, with sewn beads added. The ruff and partlet are of organdie

LEFT *Elizabethan costume made for a doll (about 35 cm – 14 in. high). The decoration of the panel includes tiny beads and fine gold painted string. The model was made from wire and strips of fabric, the head from papier mâché. Time consuming, but can be made by older children, in much the same way as making a full sized costume*

Front panel worked on dress satin, using gilded string
and cord, beads, old buckles etc. The overskirt is made from
an old yellow cotton brocade curtain covered with nylon
dress net, which had been previously gilded. (When gilding
dress net be sure to rest it on plain fabric; the gold dripping
through the holes will decorate the backing fabric, which can
then be used for something else.) The net was fixed to the
curtain fabric by free machine stitching in dark red which
added a little life to the overall dull gold effect. The pattern
round the edge of the overskirt was made by cutting out
pieces from the daubed black mull which is illustrated in the
chapter on decorated fabrics. The entire skirt was heavily
sewn with beads. This dress illustrates the vitality that can
still be obtained when using a monochrome range of rather
soft colour, simply by varying the tones and textures

LEFT *Dress based on shape often seen in German paintings (though panel is not typical). This garment, apart from the rich trimmings of panel and sleeves, is made entirely of blot dyed old sheets, mainly in sky blue and geranium pink. Given time spent on decoration, costume of this period does not necessarily demand rich fabric*

RIGHT *Close up of panel showing work in progress. This shows clearly the use of free brush work and net appliqué very freely applied (beads and jewels to be added)*

28

This dress is an adaptation of the previous one. This
version was worn by Perdita in A Winter's Tale, *the
original skirt has been removed and replaced by a dyed
cotton sheet folded in two and gathered into the bodice,
thus making an underskirt at the same time. The bodice
and sleeves covered in net and heavily embroidered with
dull gold painted string. This version is more accurately
German than the original*
   *In this version of the play the Bohemian characters wore
German costume, and the Sicilian characters contemporary
Italian costume*

LEFT *Two Italian Renaissance costumes. Woman's dress is made from bridal brocade bought in a sale, and machine embroidered with net, gold cord and beads. This is a rich and comparatively expensive garment, but given time, money and expertise, not beyond the resources of a school. Although a straight stitch machine was used, and the design freely drawn, a similar design could be produced by swing needle, and the design drawn with the aid of a template or embroidery carbon. If machine embroidery is to be used, then it is essential that the panel be decorated before being attached to the dress. The man's costume was built onto a shape which was designed on the wearer in unbleached calico, and then covered with scraps of rich material, mainly black grosgrain and white velvet, sewn in stripes, afterwards carefully sewn with pearls and jewels. For details and close up of sleeves see pages 39, 40 and 41. In contrast to some techniques we have shown, these costumes required the skill of good dressmakers*

RIGHT *Close up of panel showing peacock*

Costume for Olivia in Twelfth Night. *The skirt is a blot-dyed rayon bedspread in black, dark green and crimson, producing an overall lightable murky effect. The skirt was attached to an old evening dress which made a substantial underskirt, the top was covered in dark green and black net, trimmed with beads and string, and lightly sprayed with gunmetal paint*

31

LEFT *Costume for Lady MacDuff, the main construction in furnishing velvet, with richly embroidered sleeves and panel using fabric scraps*

RIGHT *Close-up of front panel, very many different fabric scraps and beads were used, fixed by machine and by hand, also centres of net curtain flowers, crochet doylies, and eyelet embroidery (cut from an old evening bag). This dress is extremely rich and afforded maximum creative experience for the designer. A very soft muted range of colour was used, in order to conform to the needs of the character and still have great richness*

LEFT *Back fastening of Lady MacDuff's dress, showing technique of concealing zip. Although zips are absolutely essential for quick changes, they are disturbing to the audience if visible*

RIGHT *Close-up of bodice front, showing detail of embroidery, the ruff is made of gold sprayed organdie. This in fact turned out khaki—sprays are often of limited value, though sometimes essential for last minute alterations. However, this colour accident was very successful*

33

LEFT *Venetian costume—the overskirt of the woman's dress made from furnishing fabric in raspberry red, blot dyed with orange. This device produced the kind of luminous richness associated with Venetian painting. The doublet worn by the man, is from pieces of velvet and lamé, stitched onto a calico base, with braid and fabric scraps freely applied by machine. The pants are based on a pair of men's shorts covered with satin lining, with bands of furnishing fabric*

TOP RIGHT *Close up of panel on scarlet dress satin, decorated with fabric scraps in various shades of red, beads, dyed string, buttons, curtain rings, etc. This fabric indicates that an impressionistic effect of colour and texture involving various degrees of luminosity, rather than a steady pattern, may be effective*

ABOVE RIGHT *Top of a dress in scarlet velvet, showing heavy appliqué based mainly on a string vest sprayed gold. A large variety of beads and jewels give a rich effect*

TOP LEFT *Bodice cut out and darted (made from a basic blouse pattern—to be found in nearly all pattern books). Made from cotton, blot dyed and stippled freely with a scrubbing brush dipped in various shades of green and blue. The left side shows strips of taffeta freely torn being fixed with pins for sewing*

ABOVE LEFT *Shows the panel mounted on the bodice, ready for making up and decorating*

ABOVE RIGHT *Pointed front panel showing free appliqué of net, beads, fabric scraps and broken chain, mounted on cotton and backed with heavy vilene. A stiff foundation is necessary for this part of the dress*

LEFT *Seventeenth century costume made from old fabric. No yardage was available, and this was made from the random contents of the bit box. Namely, an old loose chair cover, Terylene curtains, many pieces of lining taffeta, beads, ribbon, etc*

CENTRE *and* RIGHT *Back and front views of a late Victorian dress made from very cheap unbleached calico, the bodice and overskirt made from voile. The bodice has been made from a simple blouse pattern and trimmed with beads, buttons, lace scraps, etc, to simulate a Victorian shape. The sleeves are period lace from an old garment. Many of the frills and flounces are made from old tablecloth edging, etc. This costume indicates the possibilities of combining old and authentic, with modern and synthetic, without conflict*

Another late Victorian dress. The top is an old flock-nylon bridesmaid's dress, covered with a strip of lace from an old evening dress and decorated with thin cord. The skirt is an old lace bedspread with velvet strips inserted made from an old curtain. The sleeves are made from the broad hems of two underslips along with pieces of curtain velvet. The dress is in shades of pink and dark red, very little dressmaking required

Sleeves

One good practice we have found is to make sleeves, where appropriate, a very important feature of a costume. If these sleeves are made detachable—as was indeed the case in certain periods, especially during the Renaissance, it is possible to alter costumes from time to time, with little trouble. Sleeves from the fifteenth to the seventeenth centuries, and occasionally beyond these dates, can be composed of many tiers and layers of different materials, fixed either onto an existing garment with straight sleeves (old bodice or cardigan), or mounted on straight sleeves made from very cheap material. This not only uses up scraps, it creates a lively effect from the play of colours and different textures. The scraps can of course be dyed, and 'blot' dyeing will add to the variety of colour and texture. Beads or bits of jewelry, or other sight catching objects can be sewn or glued on, and will add to the effectiveness of the sleeves when lit.

There are many ways of constructing sleeves, we give three suggestions in our diagrams. For those who wish to keep cutting and sewing to a minimum, old frilled curtain pelmets, or ruffled curtain tops can be decorated and used effectively to make elaborate sleeves. Another useful source of sleeve material is the top of flared or fully gathered skirts from evening or cocktail dresses, especially those made of grosgrain, satin, velvet, etc. These often crop up in jumble or rummage sales. One such skirt cut in half or four, will make a good basis for a full sleeve. An existing bodice will often form the basic top of a costume, using the skirt to make full sleeves. Old coat linings frayed slightly and faded to soft subtle colours are good to use for parts of sleeves, ruched and gathered, and combined with other bits, these often look better than newly-bought, rather brash and modern looking fabrics of the same sort.

It is often difficult to convince people that old material may really be preferable to new, but we suggest that they abandon their prejudice and try effects with lighting.

Much of the movement in a play is that of gesture and arm movement. If the actors know that their arms are well dressed, this will be an encouragement to use them more eloquently.

SLEEVE 1
Scale 1:10
25mm seam allowance

SLEEVE ONE

A   Join side 1, 3 to 2, 4

Run gathering stitches from 5 to 6 and around the bottom.

B   On the wrong side, machine 25 mm (1 in.) wide tape, as shown on the diagram, keeping the stitches as close to the edge as possible, as they are to be used for threading narrow tape through. Then thread narrow tape or ribbon through the two channels, fixing firmly at the top (diagram *C*). Leaving the tape hanging at the cuff.

Now join side 1, 3 to 2, 4, then turn up the cuff about 13 mm ($\frac{1}{2}$ in.).

Now gather the bottom of diagram *A* and join to the top of diagram *B*.

Gather the top of the sleeve and attach to the bodice.

Fit onto the wearer and gently push the sleeve up by pulling the tapes and pushing at the same time. When the sleeves are the correct length, sew the tapes firmly, trim off and decorate the cuff.

ABOVE LEFT *Variation of sleeve based on diagram 1, in brown grosgrain on Italian Renaissance dress*

RIGHT *Sleeve based on diagram 1, heavy dress fabric (see page 30). Top of sleeve machine embroidered with appliqué on net, sewn with beads and jewels*

LEFT *Variation on diagram 1, blister nylon dress fabric in rich red, with freely applied strips in various red fabrics. This sleeve depends for effect on the play of light on textured surfaces, and variety of one colour. Note, the forearm is not ruched, but straight to the wrist*

*Man's doublet sleeve made from velvet and lamé,
scraps of rich fabric mounted on calico. Woman's dress as
previous illustration with ruff removed to provide Venetian
rather than Elizabethan effect*

LEFT *Sleeve based on diagram 1, using a piece of frayed fabric (damaged factory reject). The puff is made of soft nylon, with strips of fabric in off-white shades, applied at random, and subsequently held by a layer of net, fixed by machine embroidery to provide stiffness*

RIGHT *Close up of original fabric showing decorative use of fraying. With practice, faults and accidents of this kind can be used creatively*

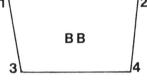

SLEEVE 2
Scale 1:10
25 mm seam allowance

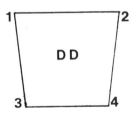

SLEEVE TWO

AA   Join side 1, 3 to 2, 4.
Gather top and bottom.
BB   Join side 1, 3 to 2, 4.
Attach *BB* to *AA*.
CC   Join side 1, 3 to 2, 4.
Gather top and bottom.
Attach to *BB*.
DD   Join side 1, 3 to 2, 4.
Attach to *CC*.
Turn up cuff and attach lace or ruff.
Join the sleeve to the bodice, then push up the sleeve
until the second puff (diagram *CC*) fits over the elbow,
allowing the arm to bend comfortably.

ABOVE LEFT *Sleeve of German style dress (see page 28) made from many multi-coloured scraps of fabric, a variation of diagram 2. This photograph shows felt scraps being stapled onto sleeve bands*

ABOVE *New version of same sleeve, the strips have been stiffened with hessian and covered with net and collage, the decorated armbands of the original covered with dark red velvet*

LEFT *Same sleeve showing wool cardigan sleeve fitted inside (see instructions for making up page 43)*

Decorated lurex stockings were attached to the bodice of this
dress and velvet puffs added top and bottom, the stockings
acting both as a tight sleeve and a decorated band. This
dress was made by an eleven year old girl in an art class
for a school production

SLEEVE 3
Scale 1:10
25mm seam allowance

**Using diagram A
and top of
diagram B
from preceeding pages**

SLEEVE THREE

Use diagram *AA* from sleeve two.

Use the top 305 mm (12 in.) of block *B* from sleeve one,
draw up to 178 mm (7 in.). Join this to the puff from
sleeve two, and make up the rest of the sleeve as in two.

NB   These sleeves when finished are approximately 914
mm (36 in.) long, and must be adjusted to fit the individual.
It is essential that the pieces between the puffs fit as tightly
as possible. A simple way to keep the sleeves tight and
puffed out, is the addition of an old woollen sleeve from a
jumper or cardigan, which must be pushed through the
sleeve before it is attached to the bodice, and then joined
onto the bodice at the same time (see page 14). It is possible
to add as many puffs as desired, by shortening the straights
accordingly.

46

LEFT *Sleeve based on diagram 3, very many different
fabric scraps. In contrast to the previous sleeves, this one
is worked and sewn meticulously (see Lady MacDuff page 32)*

RIGHT
*Sleeve made from half a skirt in heavy grey-green
grosgrain daubed with silver. The forearm is made from an
old Dutch blind (ie a ruched blind), blot dyed, with a satin
cuff. This is structurally a variation on diagram 1, that
required no pattern making because of the nature of the
materials*

ABOVE *Same sleeve showing decoration added. The harsh glitter of the cuff has been modified by means of torn strips of very old dress taffeta. Old fabrics of this kind, rotted beyond repair, though useless for major items, because of deterioration, can make a very valuable contribution to the softness and subtlety of period costumes which may offend if entirely constructed from modern synthetic fabrics.*

A colour illustration of the complete dress is shown on the back of the jacket. Sleeves made separately (see diagram on page 46 and illustration above). Bodice made separately (see page 35). Skirt panel made separately, and mounted on a blot dyed sheet. The overskirt is made from a portion of an old blue velvet curtain, faded almost to grey in places. The panel and bodice are heavily beaded and jewelled, with the addition of much free appliqué work in various fabrics including nets of various colours. The whole dress includes numerous shapes of material all old, and no two pieces of colour exactly alike. The point we are stressing here is that a harmonious effect can be obtained this way, providing the colours are subtly blended. This is a range of blues, greens, greys and yellows. By these means a very satisfying effect may be achieved, which is sometimes preferable to new bright fabric which can be tedious to the eye. This technique encourages economy in materials and creative thinking.

ABOVE *Rudimentary stage of sleeve, made strictly according to diagram 2. Using any old brocade scraps, with lurex cuff*

ABOVE *Sleeve on a calico base, quite straight and very long, made from old curtain pelmets dyed dull brown and daubed silver, with original rufflette tape causing the double puff effect. Forearm, made from a piece of gilded bedspread, cuff made from gilded lace edged tray cloth*

ABOVE RIGHT
Sleeve made from rayon brocade, originally silver and white, dyed emerald green. This sleeve is a simple shape, wide at the top, tapering to the cuff, and twice as long as the required arm length. Lack of decoration is compensated for by the play of light on deep ruching of very luminous fabric

RIGHT *Wide straight sleeve, with longer free strips fixed at cuff and gartered twice to give effect of double puff, requiring a minimum of sewing. This sleeve is in rich reds and oranges, and looks splendid under gold coat, see page 34*

LEFT *Green velvet dress with undersleeve in pale green silk made large enough to be drawn through the cut away spaces, decorated with string and velvet*

RIGHT *Close up of sleeve on page 19, tied onto shoulders over a plain sleeve of nylon jersey, decorated with net, beads, velvet scraps and braid*

50

This enormous puffed sleeve was added to an existing costume, there was no shaping required, as a complete curtain was used, heavily gathered and pleated top and bottom in an ad-hoc manner

51

LEFT *This costume is made of blanket, the pieces before sewing were overlaid with strips of multi-coloured taffetta and rags. The very long sleeves are held in place by garters*

ABOVE RIGHT *Large sleeve in traditional patterned furnishing fabric trimmed with strips of old furnishing velvet for this fifteenth-century robe*

ABOVE LEFT *An old table runner in gold crushed velvet makes this collar for a black velvet cloak over matching tunic with huge embroidered sleeves striped with torn and frayed fabric strips of dull gold lining fabric, embroidered with dark yellow thread and string*

ABOVE *Black velvet tunic, late fifteenth century, with collar of gold painted felt, trimmed with string, beads and fabric scraps. The effect of the shirt protruding from the sleeves is faked, the sleeve is in fact all in one including cuffs*

ABOVE RIGHT *Original dressing-gown, rejected when ruined by hair dye*

RIGHT *Doublet in course of construction*

ABOVE
Doublet inspired by Titian painting, and made from a dyed quilted housecoat. Blue blot dyeing covers up original flower sprigs. The width of the puff has been achieved by slitting the original sleeves, and inserting strips cut from the skirt

RIGHT *Sleeves made of blanket with strips of taffetta lining laid on top. The sleeve is very long and fixed by garters or rubber bands. The cuffs are heavily collaged and gilded. The jewel hanging from gold painted sizal string is made from old lino blocks painted gold*

OPPOSITE TOP LEFT *Sleeves with alternating puffs of old curtain fabric, picked out in gold and decorated with beads. This costume indicates once again, that yardage is not necessary in great quantity to make an effective costume, provided the dressmaker has patience and ingenuity*

OPPOSITE TOP RIGHT *Long wide sleeve gathered at elbow with braid, and with deep tucks down the forearm. This sleeve was designed to use several scraps of rich material in the absence of full yardage*

OPPOSITE BELOW *Sleeve shown being attached to doublet by means of eyelet holes*

LEFT
Shirt as worn under many tunics in this book. Very full white rayon jersey. This fabric is unbeatable for soft drape effects needing a certain amount of body

RIGHT
German doublet, using quilted coat lining with rich surface embroidery in red and white. The sleeves are dyed calico with felt scraps and padded decoration. The sword is made from filed aluminium, good for decoration, but not for heavy fighting

Jewelry and headgear

Polythene lids, bottle tops, tin lids, cord and string, sealing wax, gold, silver and copper powder, *Marvin Medium*, black or sepia dye, paint or ink; chocolate and sweet containers; beads and costume jewelry, felt tabs, scraps of leather, thick cloth and hessian, clear glue, cheap chain, leather thonging, small metal articles of all kinds, old lino blocks, paint sprays, feathers of all kinds (including feather cuttings, feather dusters, layered feather hats), foam rubber, nylon and hair switches, milliners' canvas, wire and many other similar items.

Making stage jewelry can be a creative task for a whole group, or it can serve well as a spare time or interim activity, when a child finishes another piece of work early. It is easy to organise at home, needing little space. Though it may be desirable to have a certain unity in the work, scope can always be given for enterprising and imaginative use of materials, and for an individual's inspired improvisation.

It is important at the outset to study form. Eighteenth century girandoles will need different treatment from Celtic torques or Byzantine plaques. Nothing looks odder than glittering, many-faceted jewels on ancient Greeks. Facet cutting is a fairly late invention, and in many cases, a general impression of cabochon gems or garnet and glass, *cloisonné*, or wrought gold and slabs of lapis lazuli may be what is needed.

Here as with the fabrics, there is no need for slavish copying, as long as the general principles are borne in mind. The distance and lighting will produce half the illusion, and creative improvisation may be better than dogged imitation.

ABOVE *Necklace of dyed* Marvin Medium *dried solid (the dye was dripped into the liquid medium before it began to solidify). Small beads were added, and the pieces strung together on fine thread*

LEFT *Bracelet made from scraps found in a work box, including paper-clips, hooks and eyes, necklace fastener, etc, plus broken Christmas baubles, and strands of pulled rubber solution*

ABOVE Collar with centre piece of corroded metal (found on building site), the holes in the metal made it easy to sew onto a piece of fabric, adding beads at the same time. The rest made from felt and other stiff fabric, trimmed with buttons, painted silver and sewn with pearls and small beads

RIGHT Wide collar incorporating the narrower collar above. The original collar was fairly delicate, and when it began to disintegrate it was attached to a new collar and repainted silver and light gold with additional decoration

59

ABOVE LEFT *Selection of collars based on heavy blanket or felt, trimmed with small metal objects, beads, string, curtain rings, etc*

ABOVE *Large collar made from crochet table mat, with the centre cut out. This was painted gold, and laid on black felt. Heavily decorated with off-cuts of the crochet mat, silver painted dried leaves, curtain rings, broken chain necklaces, etc.*

LEFT *Collar on gold painted fabric. The main decoration is a lino block which had been previously used for print making in school, this has been painted gold, and beads, buttons, etc have been freely added. (Never throw old lino blocks away)*

OPPOSITE ABOVE *Collar made from old blanket and felt scraps, painted various tones of gold, with buttons, beads, curtain rings, string collage, and squares of blue lurex fabric (painted over with ink).*

OPPOSITE RIGHT *Detail of necklace above*

LEFT *Smaller collar made from the piece cut from the centre of the aforementioned crochet mat. Painted in various shades of gold, heavily decorated with buttons and string*

RIGHT *Large gold collar, very heavily decorated with string, beads, pen nibs, etc, and several layers of dripped Marvin Medium (and pva paste will do). This collar was dipped in dark green dye and repainted to give the effect of richness and age*

Gold collar based on felt, trimmed with string, dripped glue and Marvin Medium, *curtain rings, beads and metal scraps*

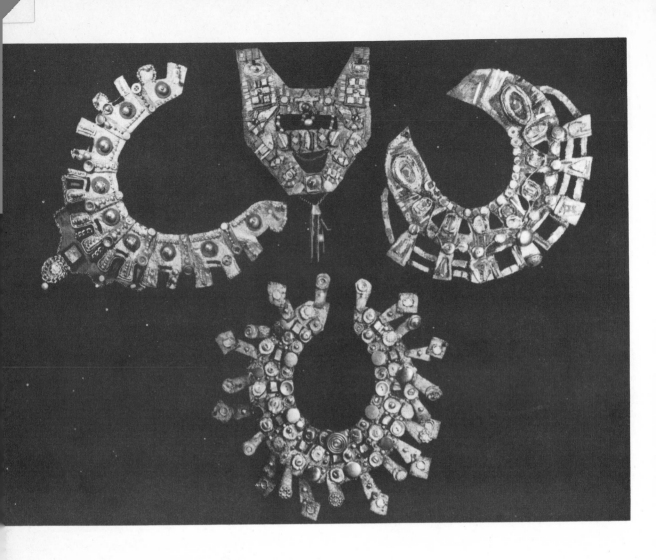

Group of collars made by children as part of an art and dance project, made from felt, blanket, buttons, beads, etc. Bright colours on gold and silver painted fabric. Theme Aztec

ABOVE *Large collar, made on pleated linen, sewn with felt strips and string collage, button trimmed, painted light and dark gold. Beads and black ink added*

RIGHT *Pendant made from polythene lid sewn with beads, buttons, etc, mounted on gold-painted neckband of fabric. Made in school for a Greek play*

*Two groups of items made for Norse Warriors.
String, beer bottle tops, dressmaker's weights, metallic
fabrics, beads, cardboard, various metal items, an old lino
block, leather thonging, polythene lid, canvas, etc*

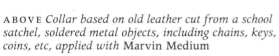

ABOVE *Collar based on old leather cut from a school
satchel, soldered metal objects, including chains, keys,
coins, etc, applied with* Marvin Medium

RIGHT *Collar based on gold painted fabric with small
slabs of lino wired through. The lino is coloured with
various metallic powders in* Marvin Medium. *Beads and
fabric added*

ABOVE LEFT *Egyptian collar on black and turquoise felt, heavily decorated with gold painted felt strips, string, pen nibs and beads. The long chains centre front hang to the knees of the wearer – creating interesting movement.*

LEFT *Egyptian head-dress, made from strips of felt attached to an old tight fitting hat, some of the strips were plaited and weighted with gold felt and beads. The hair decoration is made from a thin gilt snake bracelet plus an amber coloured string of glass beads*

ABOVE RIGHT *on opposite page and* ABOVE
*Demonstration of head-dress built up from four black
nylon switches, with bird pelt centre-piece (covering
hairgrips and join), beads, various feathers.
No preliminary work required. Ear-rings made from tassels
from old feather boa attached to existing pair. Necklace
from old beads and chains*

RIGHT *Head-dress made with chicken wire and various
kinds of swarf (metal turnings)*

LEFT *Helmet made from chicken wire, coarsely woven with great variety of torn fabrics (some metalised), with buckles, beads, etc. Tassels made from dyed unspun wool. Tunic of coarse fabric, with collage of dyed blanket, beads, cord, etc*

RIGHT *A lightly stuffed nylon stocking attached to an old hat is the basis of this turban head-dress with crown style points. The gilded and heavily jewelled crown has a wrap round hood which may be arranged according to taste for any of the Three Kings*

ABOVE LEFT *Crown mounted on plastic band using items rejected from other work, including broken combs, plastic building kit pieces, small bottle brush, buttons, twigs and plastic flowers*

RIGHT *Crown on wire frame, fabric stiffened with* Marvin Medium. *Decoration of wood-shavings, plastic prisms, leather thonging, beads, buttons, broken glass, etc*

LEFT *Head-dress made on a band previously used for stiffening a hat, decorated with feathers, plastic leaves, beads etc*

ABOVE *Head-dress made on existing hat-band; feathers, beads and buttons*

OPPOSITE TOP LEFT Gold, Frankincense and Myrrh. *Made from a toffee tin and two wine bottles (extended with toilet-roll cores), decorated with beads, string, beer bottle tops, polythene lid, gold paint. All glued with* Marvin Medium. *(See page 16)*

OPPOSITE CENTRE LEFT *Cornucopia made from cardboard cone, extended with glued screwed paper, and finally layered with tissue paper. Decorated with pins, twigs, beads, wood shavings, dead leaves, etc*

OPPOSITE BOTTOM LEFT *Fan of assorted feathers. The centre is made from the bottom of a brass-wire fruit basket, and the handle from the rim of the same basket. Brooch pinned to centre. Held together with soft wire*

ABOVE RIGHT *Goblet made from cardboard carton with plastic leaves and flowers, shells, beads, etc painted gold*

ABOVE LEFT *Crown made from the sides of the wire basket as used for the fan. Trimmed with diamanté, beads, wire, etc*

BELOW LEFT *Mediaeval head-dress made from wire and plastic foam, covered with painted millinery canvas. Decorated with sequins, beads and braid.*

ABOVE RIGHT *and* OPPOSITE LEFT *Mediaeval head-dresses made from millinery canvas, covered with fabric scraps, beads, etc, and chiffon drapes. The chiffon was bought very cheaply on a market stall*

ABOVE RIGHT *Crown made from wire covered with gold fabric, with beads and buckles added*

BELOW RIGHT *Bonnet made from the stiffening inside an old hat, as part of a test in creating headgear from old rubbish and throw away objects. This is painted gold and trimmed with beads and fabric*

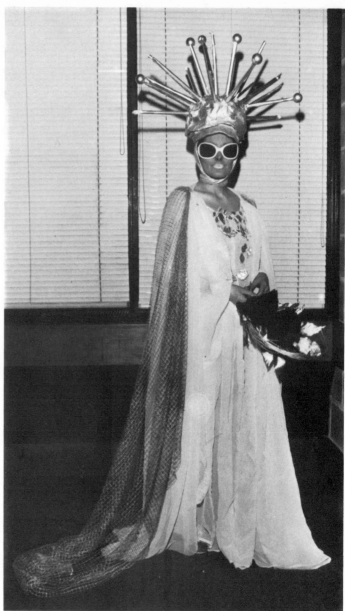

LEFT *Typical head-dress for our production of* Twelfth
Night, *rolled headband (stuffed nylon stockings would do
very well), tying at the back with ribbons, trimmed with
braid and flowers. For details of this type of head-dress see
early sixteenth century portraits*

ABOVE *Space Bride. Head-dress made from newspaper
tubes attached to an old scarf hat, and trimmed with table
tennis balls, the whole thing painted silver. Dress made
from several heavy nylon curtains, the train from gold and
silver painted curtain net. The dress is decorated with
silver foil and painted string*

ABOVE *and* RIGHT
Head-dress of gilded corrugated card trimmed with braid, feathers, buttons, etc. This was made very rapidly

Leather and armour

A good way of simulating leather, especially gold and silver leather, is to take some scraps of wool or cotton jersey, the better the quality the better the effect. The fabric may be dyed or not as wished. A fairly thick coat of gold or silver powder in *Marvin Medium*, should be applied to the fabric so as to seep well into the grain. If worn and eroded effects are desired, the piece may be screwed into a lump, or two pieces of fabric may be glued together, face to face, and left to dry. The *Marvin Medium* will toughen the fabric and set the gold or colour. Finally, take the stiffened fabric, and pull it about, separating the grain, or pull the two glued faces apart, or disentangle the bundle. The creasing or gluing may cause patches of different colour and texture to appear, flakes of the hardened gold film may peel off, and all will add to the richness of the texture. Do not throw away such flakes, they will be useful for other fabrics, jewelry or collage. The result looks very much like coarse, worn or richly gilded leather, and is very suitable for armour, tunics, surfacing shields, loin aprons and so on, including all kinds of fantastic costumes.

The use of simulated leather is especially suitable for armour. The principles we have mentioned again and again should be noted—lively and rich textured effects light best.

Many people will be familiar with mail made from coarse dishcloth fabric, or knitted from string, and we feel that we need not enlarge on this, beyond saying once again that silver nickel powder in *Marvin Medium* or *Binder D*, may prove better and cheaper than the usual daubed or sprayed lacquer.

As already mentioned, fantastic armour may be assembled happily from all kinds of junk, using hessian, calico or blanket as a base, in the form of a tunic, tabard or leotard.

A usual method of making plate armour is to soak felt in size, mould the shapes to the body and paint these. Felt yardage is however, very expensive, and old, closely-woven woollen cloth (blanket, old coats, etc.) may prove preferable.

Simple knitted helmet of string, painted silver with powder in Helizarin Binder D. Marvin Medium *may be used, but this type of garment is better if flexible*

Costume from The Bacchae, *calico tunic with sewn
pieces of various metalised fabrics (gold, bronze and silver
powder in* Marvin Medium, *with fabric colours showing
through), mainly brown. On the surface, smaller pieces of
gold painted fabric, old brooches, etc, glued with* Marvin
Medium. *The edges of the garment bound with cord. The
tunic lined with sheet wadding (old quilted dressing-gown
will do), goes over a pleated cambric skirt. An attempt was
made here to produce an impression of Greek armour, but to
retain an abstract effect. The cloak is dark blue woollen
jersey, edges left raw but neatened with pinking shears, as
fabric hangs and drapes better with no hems and as few
seams as possible. The sword was forged from an iron bar,
and the hilt cast in bronze from a wooden pattern (not
beyond the scope of a boys' metalwork department)*

OPPOSITE ABOVE *Group of children wearing Greek costume in a wide variety of colours produced by blot dyeing old sheets. The armour in the foreground is a collage of various fabrics, mostly rich metallic effects, on old blanket.. The tunic skirts are strips of dyed sheet attached under the armour at the waist, and block printed with potato or lino. The printing, collage and the making of jewelry, for a cast of ninety children aged between eleven and sixteen, was made by children in art classes*

OPPOSITE BELOW *Detail of costume*

ABOVE *Greek costumes, using old sheets dyed orange, pink and blue, with simple printing and added jewelry. The armour tunic was originally made to fit a schoolgirl, this kind of garment can easily be adjusted to fit most sizes, if a generous wrap over is allowed at the back. The skirt can be lengthened to suit the wearer*

RIGHT *Two girls wearing armour on basic tunics made from an old tablecloth. The tunics were decorated with collage in a wide variety of fabrics, including dyed blankets painted with size, cuttings of leather, sheet and blanket edges, and gold and silver painted scraps of fabric*

LEFT *Breast plate for Merlin from* Thor with Angels. *The basic fabric is a piece of reject batik heavily waxed and firm to sew. Metalised fabric, many metal objects, and a quantity of string have been applied with* Marvin Medium. *The boss was originally a round chocolate pack padded from the back to give weight and stability, and then decorated. The accidental green-bronze colour of the basic fabric, suited this character well*

RIGHT *Piece torn from the inside of a wax lined sack (for packing paraffin wax) and painted gold, this fabric could be very useful for corroded armour and war gear*

LEFT *Abstract shield made from squashed wire,
coarsely woven with numerous fabrics and string, with
decoration of broken glass*

RIGHT *Swords and scabbards, simply but heavily
decorated with string and small metal objects. The blades
are beaten tin over wood, and the scabbards are made of
cardboard. We strongly advise that swords be metal or
metal coated, not wood or plastic. Rapiers and broadswords
may be made from filed aluminium, but they are not advised
for practical fights as they buckle easily. If all else fails, hire
the weapons*

ABOVE *Breast plate made from chicken wire covered with newspaper, sprayed black, green and gold for an impressionistic metallic effect. This close-up shows detail of making, but the effect when worn is intended to be blurred by distance. This technique is not really suitable for any performance involving close contact between actors and audience*

LEFT *Helmet made from chicken wire, layered with newspaper and Marvin Medium. The crest is polystyrene, bound to a cardboard form with tissue paper and paste. Painted with Marvin Medium and gold powder (do not use a spray, this dissolves the polystyrene). The helmet is a silver gilt colour, with blue patches, unevenly daubed, to avoid a garish effect. The spear has a wooden shaft and a tin blade, dulled with black paint to make it look more substantial. The shield is cardboard, with a collage of torn net curtains coated in Marvin Medium, unevenly daubed with gold and silver. The cow device (representing Thebes) was built with cardboard shapes*

ABOVE *Inside of metal breastplate showing fastenings and felt re-inforcements down centre*

RIGHT *Metal breast plate, tin snipped to form darts and bolted to form curves, made from white metal, sprayed black, green and gold*

Peasant costumes

Clothing minor characters may be a very simple job, or it may be the most difficult and elaborate of all. Non-speaking lords and ladies often account for the greatest labour (and opportunity) in a costume play. St Joan, except for her armour, can be dressed in half an hour. A useful standard collection of oddments, for beginning the work of dressing peasants and the like, is as follows:

Old trousers

(trews, jeans, etc.) These can be cut down to form knee-breeches or long Elizabethan slops, or used short to act as a base for Elizabethan round hose—with the big advantage that they fit the characters with ease (especially if they have supplied their own garments). Be careful about fly-fastenings, it may be necessary to 'fake' flat fronts or cod-pieces.

Old socks

especially thick wool socks of plain dark colours (avoiding nylon), are invaluable for simulating soft shoes of all kinds. With length added to the toes they become mediaeval, with added laces and decoration, and with broad toe padding they do very well for tudor shoes, sprayed or painted with silver they do for mail shoes. Wear them over plimsolls for 'body'. Ordinary leather shoes on the whole, are too heavy for stage use, they tend to inhibit movement.

Old shirts

These with collars removed and 'pie frills' added for Tudor characters, or, for Renaissance men, bishop sleeves are effective.

ABOVE LEFT *Sixteenth century ruffians, dressed quickly from odd items. Cut down trousers, dyed long underwear, socks over plimsolls, odd leather belts, worn shirts with frilled collars, old jumpers, tunics made from old blanket. All of these items were rapidly dyed in earth-coloured dye, which produced a variety of black, brown and green shades*

LEFT *Serving man and woman from* Macbeth, *wearing old shirts extended with bishop sleeves, with cuffs and pie frills added. The tunic made from oddments of fabric, dyed various browns. The woman is wearing cap made on the head, jumper with pie frills and cuffs added, skirt made from dyed bedspread, with calico apron. These garments were made rapidly from the very last remaining items, and they contrasted well in a range of rust, scarlet, green and mustard, with the richness of the principals' costumes*

Men's long underwear

(Long johns) These homely garments—sometimes cotton jersey, preferably wool—may sometimes be begged from neighbours and relatives, or bought fairly cheaply. Dyed, they make good tights, worn under hip-length tunics or doublets. They may be effectively cross-gartered, or simply worn with plimsolls under thick socks, rolled down. Modern stretch nylon tights tend to cling too closely, and are often too transparent. If tights are being bought, wool or cotton serve better, white cotton tights dyed are comparatively cheap. If only nylon tights are available, it is often a good idea to wear two pairs for thickness.

Thick woollen sweaters

These may be worn (having been previously dyed to 'blur' the surface and disguise the look of modernity) under tunics either sleeveless or wide sleeved, for either men or women.

When making costumes for female servants in Tudor plays, we have used sweaters with puffs added at the shoulders and ruffs or collars at the necks. If a tight fitting sweater is used the effect is quite adequate provided a fairly gathered skirt is worn over the jumper, and an apron tied over that. In such cases, the jumper-bodice should be stiffened, because a natural bosomy look is alien to Tudor style (study books of drawings and portraits). By omitting the puffs and ruffs, and fixing the skirt over the hip line, a more mediaeval effect may be obtained.

The universal old sheet may be pressed into service again for aprons, wimples or Tudor bonnets—a glance at a Dürer painting of humble women will give many ideas for twisting the fabric to make such caps, they simply need folding and pleating into shape over a headband, and pinning or sewing. Such articles may easily be blotched and dirtied, tattered and otherwise artistically deranged where suitable. It is sometimes a good idea to take the edge off glistening whiteness, especially where peasants are to be contrasted with court characters in white. Unbleached calico or twill is quite effective, as are old sacks for working aprons.

TOP RIGHT *Mistress Quickly and serving wench, wearing blot dyed heavy furnishing fabric, hessian and old curtains, in a range of warm pinks and browns, with items of haberdashery in calico*

RIGHT *This dress in its original state can be seen in the background on the left of the* Macbeth *banqueting scene (opposite). This was later converted for* Twelfth Night, *largely by means of dyed net curtains and furnishing taffetta, the new skirt was attached above the natural waistline and the ruff and partlet were removed*

Sacks and blankets are the most useful articles for the making of tunics, either T-shaped or simple sleeveless bags, and for skirts. Often the more dirty and tatty the better— these items going on from year to year, getting more and more wretched, sometimes turn out to be the most effective and lightable of all. We advocate blot dyeing in shades of sepia, olive, and all kinds of dirty grey and black.

Odd shapes of the same material, slung by means of a cord, serve well for cloaks, or they can be made to just fit the shoulders by gathering into a band that fastens across the chest.

Thick cord, old leather belts or dull looking chains can serve as fastenings. Monks are easily habited in this kind of gear, though they tend to require more yardage.

The drab, muted colours of these articles allow for endless re-combinations, fitting in with a wide variety of plays, and a brighter detail may be occasionally added, especially if a *Book of Hours* or Mediaeval manuscript is being used as inspiration.

OPPOSITE ABOVE
Group of peasants dressed in remnants of old sheets and curtains in colours taken from fresco paintings. These were the rude mechanicals in an Italianate production of A Midsummer Night's Dream

OPPOSITE BELOW
Group of children dressed in old sheets and remnants, in earth colours, worn over jumpers, tights and socks

ABOVE RIGHT
Fifteenth century peasant, wearing a calico skirt attached to an old jumper. The stretching of the jumper has produced a long line, in contrast to the high waist of the court lady, since it might be supposed that the peasant fashions lagged behind. Though simple, this dress in yellow, green and pink worked well with the court dresses. In this play, The Lark, *we dyed all the peasant linen slightly yellow to contrast with the pure white garments of the Dominican monks. Wimples of this sort need not be made-up beforehand, but can be rapidly improvised on the night*

RIGHT
Eighteenth century country girl's costume, made up as follows: Straight wide skirt made from an old sheet, blot dyed and gathered at the waist, over a scoop-necked jumper. Cuffs and fichu made separately from net curtain. Panniers from strip of dyed sheet, gathered at the waist, hitched up and pinned, apron made from sheeting. The bonnet is the bottom of an old frilled petticoat, gathered at the crown

Those playing murderers and other heavy character parts, usually delight in adding detail to sleazy detail of their costumes, and willingly black their teeth and tear their clothes, and hunt around for suitable knives, etc.

After every play, it is best to collect carefully as many humble items of this sort as possible—rough wooden crosses, cords, belts, carefully whittled daggers, leather wallets made from old stachels, rusty chains, patchwork bundles, shepherds crooks, plain steel knives, roughly trimmed staffs, broken stoneware crocks, and items of copper or pewter.

Basic peasants can be transformed into common soldiers by the addition of knitted mail items, leaving the work and materials available for noblemen's armour.

Greek, Roman and Near Eastern peasants need approximately the same treatment, with perhaps lighter weight material and occasionally sandals over bare feet. Modern sandals, however simple, seldom look right, especially if made of PVC or simulated leather. Cords twisted round the ankle from a simple sole, are better. Mediterranean sailors, naked to the waist and barefoot, may be characterised by the odd ear-ring and a bundle, with a knife in the folds of the loincloth. For this purpose, old ragged, coarse-woven tablecloths or bedspreads (especially striped) can be used, the older and thinner the material has worn, the better they drape.

Some of the muted earth colours, worn with real feeling for movement, and well lit may be very beautiful indeed, however old and worn the fabric. At all cost, avoid the tell-tale shine of plastic, unless some dramatic point is being made here. Avoid also, borrowed academic gowns for mediaeval scholars, they *look* like the staff's second best.

Be careful about spectacles! If worn by mediaeval and later, but not modern, characters they should be round and nose-perched, Flemish painters are a marvellous source of ideas.

An effective group of revellers can be ruined if the serving girls are using an obvious plastic tray. Many ordinary items will serve for Greek and Roman goblets if they are painted, and decorations are added, but do look at the original sources, Greek vases are perhaps the most useful for this. All these details are obvious, but they are of paramount importance, and they really do make the difference between tattiness and quality.

Long gown of heavy woollen material, trimming from an old fur coat

*Late Victorian music hall costume, based on
a polo necked jumper, with addition of frilly false front, the
skirt is the underskirt of an evening dress, with a frill made
of cheap lining taffeta. The feather boa is authentic, and
the hat has been built up with feathers, artificial flowers
and a veil, on an old straw shape*

Decorated leotards

A simple leotard—nylon or cotton jersey, may form the basis for a quite elaborate costume. The tight skin provides an anchor for disguises of all kinds, and may be worn under any garment as a sure way of holding firmly cloaks or Greek drapery, thus avoiding much fitting and dressmaking.

To use leotards frankly as practice dress with period or characteristic items added, sometimes during the action of a play or dance, is a well known device. It serves well in girls' schools, when the task of making up a believable Victorian gentleman is clearly impossible. Not every play will take this treatment well. It is particularly useful for improvisation, and ad-libbing on a theme, or 'skeleton' dramatic structure, or for plays in which, like *King Lear* the characters are archetypes. It is a good deal less suitable for formal productions of Wilde or Chekov. However, if a play has to be done well in a very short time, it may be a better solution than ill-made, undetailed costumes, and much more creative than hiring.

Plain leotard and tights with masks. These made on wire frames layered with papier mâché, finally painted and decorated. The beards are made from fringing

LEFT *The same basic garments with the following added—
'Aztec' masks, made from simple heavy paper shapes, with
collage of metallic wrapping papers, and extra trimmings of
beads, fringe, rags and feathers. The aprons are fabric
scraps with collage decoration, and the jewelry made from
fabric, etc (a close up can be seen on page 64). This
was an intergroup project in a secondary school. The masks
were made by second year children, the aprons by third year
children and the collars by fourth years. This was part of an
art/dance project involving thirty children*

RIGHT *The same girls, this time without their tights, wearing
quickly draped pieces of dyed chiffon. The head-dresses are
made from feathers, twigs, beads, etc, and the cornucopia
is illustrated on page 73. When using plastic flowers, we
have found it best to split these and re-assemble them, as
they tend to look rather crude when used whole. It is a pity
to ignore them, as so many are available, but care is needed*

LEFT *Leotard and tights sprayed gold on top of previous gold painting. Spray alone will sink into the fabric and look dull, but it is very useful to add a final sheen. It is best to paint leotards on a model, as they stiffen slightly, and it can be difficult to stretch them into shape*

RIGHT *Same leotard hung with torn rags in a wide range of dull colours and worn with nylon hair switches, and a wire and paper bird mask*

LEFT *This costume, using a very wide range of torn dyed rags, was based on vest and briefs which had been previously dyed, but a leotard or swimming costume are equally good as foundations. These torn rags give a good effect in movement*

RIGHT *Angel with torn rag wings, mounted on a halter of gold painted fabric*

It is important to remember that the techniques mentioned in this book may be integrated with other work in the field of creative arts and should not be thought of as applicable only to the making of costumes for plays.

When applied to costume, such techniques as collage, dyeing, printing and embroidery are essentially decorative. The value of the image, where this exceeds decoration, comes when the costume is seen in movement and inter-action with others, in imaginative lighting. The work then certainly transcends in value anything that has been done in the art room or wardrobe section. There is much to be said for the view that figurative art, these days, is found at its best on the stage, especially in some of the latest experiments with movement, costumes and lighting.

In the school art room or creative work areas, work done for its own sake, while it may use many of the same methods, *must stand up by itself*. The use of embroidery and fabric printing, and other fabric crafts, mainly for decoration, however beautiful, has led to a feeling that these materials are *essentially decorative*, and cannot be used for more profound purposes. We would like to urge that this is a mistaken idea, and that fabrics and related materials may be used as effectively as paint or stone, by children and adults for the expression of equally profound visual ideas. These materials need not be restricted to a narrow range: stone and fabric, clay and fabric, fabric and heavy junk, and any or all of these combined with lights and mechanical movements are feasible and valuable in art education.

Titania and Bottom from A Midsummer Night's Dream. *Titania's costume has been improvised over a decorated leotard*